REGARDING WOMEN

REGARDING WOMEN

Poems by Barry Spacks

Cherry Grove Collections

Published by Cherry Grove Collections
P.O. Box 541106
Cincinnati, OH 45254-1106

Typeset in Goudy Old Style by WordTech Communications LLC,
Cincinnati, OH

ISBN: 1932339299
LCCN: 2003112502

Poetry Editor: Kevin Walzer
Business Editor: Lori Jareo

Visit us on the web at www.cherry-grove.com

Cover Art:
Vermeer, Johannes (1632-1675) Dutch
"Girl Interrupted at her Music," c. 1660 (DETAIL)
© The Frick Collection, New York

ACKNOWLEDGMENTS

Many of these poems first appeared, some in earlier form, in *Agnieszka's Dowery*, *American Poetry Review*, *Art Life*, *Ascent*, *The Berkeley Poetry Review*, *Blue Moon Review*, *The Boston Phoenix*, *The Bridge*, *Caffeine Destiny*, *Chelsea*, *Confrontation*, *The Cumberland Poetry Review*, *5-Trope*, *For Poetry*, *Hubbub*, *The Hudson Review*, *Image Magazine*, *Indiana Review*, *Into the Teeth of the Wind*, *Light Year*, *The Manhatten Poetry Review*, *Mudfish*, *The New Criterion*, *The New York Times*, *Ontario Review*, *Painted Hills Review*, *Pinchpenny*, *Poetry*, *Plains Poetry Journal*, *Poetry Express*, *Poetry Northwest*, *Red Weather*, *Sewanee Review*, *Solo*, *Southern Humanities Review*, *Southern Ocean Review*, *Spectrum*, *Tar River Poetry*, *Texas Quarterly*, *Two-River View*, *Whiskey Island*, *Zipzap*, *Zuzu Petals* and *Zone 3*.

"To a Lady" and "The Legend of Kuan Yin" appeared in *Teaching the Penguins to Fly*, Godine, 1975; "The Muse" in *The Company of Children*, Doubleday, 1969; "Plants on a Windowshelf" in *Brief Sparrow*, Illuminati, 1988; "Low-Budget Film" in *Something Human*, Harper's Magazine Press, 1972.

for Kimberley

CONTENTS

"'The words stenciled on the box mean 'Fragile,' but literally say, 'Use a little heart.'"

—Maxine Hong Kingston, *The Woman Warrior*

"Shiva is capable of creation only when united with Shakti. Otherwise he is just inert matter."

—*Hymn to the Devil*

I.

A BEGINNING

On the beach near dusk our bodies cast long shadows.
A troupe of sandpipers faced down the wind
and small, fearless, its ease like faith,
a white bird bobbed far out on the water.

We had no need for games or speech.
You'd shown such grandeur even then
I made blind Milton's line refer
to "she for God and he for God in her."

Next morning came a dragon sun,
the eyes within its fury yours,
blue peace within that burning's rage,
and I gave myself there, like a white bird riding.

LITTLE THINGS

for Stephen Tapscott

The great professor, quoting us Rilke:
"You must change your life," and the weight
of tears wrenched from his listeners.

Afterwards, in winter dusk,
a pregnant woman asked for my arm
to cross the square. "Such slippery snow!"

She must have seemed my mother then,
my lover now, so long it's been.
Little things...little things...

audible sobs in a lecture room
and all of us, for a time, at least,
all of us, totally changed.

LITANY

We dwell with those once touched by hand or mind:
a marriage, some long misery of lust,
a chance remark, a moving smile survive
—a gentled face, a funny sigh—
perhaps of someone never seen again
on this mere earth
where everything begun
continues, a sort of litany.

A kindness, a brief glance along the street,
keeps speaking down the years
and years and miles away
still stirs another life
to make reply.

A LINE FROM MARY MACLANE

"I love my shoes!"

—I, MARY MACLANE

I love mine too, Mary,
yet but for you
would I think to say so?

Your voice urged me,
first in the shower,
then again in bed, declaring:

"Why not enter a room full of people
and cry out for once the total truth?—
'delighted to see you! I love my shoes!'"

IN A FUNKY MOTEL

A basketball bounces at 2 a.m.,
pings off the hoop...again...again....
Next door a girl with two—at least—men
grunts, is chased, giggles...sad.

I save up the sounds of funky motels:
cricket-whirr in country places,
honest laugh now and then, pour
of a hard-earned shower...mainly it's semi's

pounding the highway...slam of car doors...
click of high heels on paving, angry
voices; later the creaking of lust-beds,
TVs selling themselves to sleep,

farting, flushing, blasts of so-called
music—"Sound," said a Holy Man,
"all of sound is mantra," not
to be praised nor blamed, bemoaned, the seethe,

roar of want and counter-want,
yes, okay, but I'll think a while
on the basketball, is it safely in bed
with its night-blooming bouncer by now? and of

the stifled pain of the woman weeping,
trying not to be heard through this thinness
of wall as morning aspires toward light
near Greenville, in a funky motel.

INNERBIRD

This bird, this Innerbird—she means you well,
but clenches in at times so very small
she's hard, tight, an acorn, a stomach pain...

in other moods you feel her fluttering
like the purple wide-sleeved garment of a queen,
frantic within you, a wild queen's will

stirring your farthest reaches till you scheme
to set her free. That wish leads you to know
you're her idea: this bird invented you;

your purposes and due-dates are her trap,
her cage of concepts, arbitrary as a map
holding Montenegro, Montana, to one special place.

Go transparent. Disappear. And then the bird's released.
But never give that unbound bird your name
or again she's small within you, seed within a cell.

Your absence lets her soar forth at her will.
At last she has no wrappings but the air
and sweeps out hugely, and is everywhere.

LOCATING FREEDOM

"A bird is born to fly, a man,"
wrote Innocent the Third, grim Pope,
"to labor." (*Woes of the Human Condition*).

"Oh, gloomy doom," a woman teases—
"another love-earner's panting self-pity
when all in the world he desires is ballet!"

By the light of her smile I locate freedom:
one-eighth-inch past self concern.
There beautiful Others are telling their stories,

inklings inextricably mixed,
glint of specifics that time pours through
like startled sunlight through crazed glass.

No longer a clone, a motorized mourner
who envies Pan and the punch of Picasso,
I'd burn so fully I'd leave no ash.

Percussionists...how they mean to continue!
Marie Curie, sifting her pitchblend
for grains of radiance, ton after ton!

Not by the massive cathedral door
may we enter...by the small door, set
in the big one.

MILES DAVIS PLAYS "SKETCHES FROM SPAIN"

His trumpet insinuates
an amber bellydancer
who works her spine aglow
like softly burnished
Egyptian gold.

But then somehow
America approaches:
t-t-tat, little
Thirteen Colony
drum and bugle corps:

Day of the Game, bugle-brash-Saturday...
ah, that night, in lumpy Chevy,
blond-headed cowlick football hero
soothes his cheerleader; they risk all:
backseat breathmist curtains car-windows

and round comes the sinuous trumpet again,
lovers translated to tendriling swirls,
meandering silks of bodiful knowing,
brazen langour,
music from Spain.

MODEL AT THE DRAWING CLASS

Line of her neck...turn of her shoulder...
because we gaze
she's beautiful.

She lies there like a pond in spring
that suffers all night
the stars without moving.

Within the pose she's force, not thing;
each muscle whispers
its separate name—

glassed-in gorilla, throwing a tire;
anemone
opening, closing.

LOVERS MEDITATING

They focused on a candle's flame and sought
the one embrace where nothing else exists,

but each became the other's only thought,
impassioned meditators, joined at last.

Ignored by them, the candlelight persists:
the source of the great shadow that they cast.

PLANTS ON A WINDOWSHELF

I see the pleasure my neighbor takes
raising her plants, the exacting care,
teasing the tendrils up the stakes,
greeting them over coffee each morning
all lined up in the sunniest window,
ficus, shefalaria,
each in its pot...heart-shaped ivy...
side by side, like kids organized,
as hers might have been many years before,
mugging their differences at the camera.

LOW-BUDGET FILM

A boy with balloons descends along
the windows of the dorm, knocks
on the glass, a girl arrives, buys
a balloon, and as he hands it off
naturally he sinks; another
smiles, buys, till he holds at last
a single balloon to keep him afloat
and to that final window comes
the loveliest girl in the world.

THE LEGEND OF KUAN YIN

The icons show her, male, female,
many-armed. The legend goes
that wanting force she swore a vow:
May my body crack the day I fail
a single needy being! Of course
she failed, and in her brokenness
became herself, for from the thousand
fissures where her very body
cracked from willing mercy grew
the thousand arms
and thousand hands
of compassion.

II.

TREE IN A BOWL

Within its curve, a reducing mirror,
the bowl on my table reflects a tree
and the field out the window, so small and still
I enter there
where nothing changes,
leaving the pain of music, of all
that passes, and we haven't met
or loved yet, aren't
even born,
as I move
toward the small
dark tree.

WATCHING THE SOAPS

She stands by the sink, an almost naked
onion in her hand, and attends
to The Wife, The Shameless Office Girl,
The Angry Suitor, The Sexy Friend,
their words in rough translation naming
"love," that seeks transparency:
an open face, a latchless door...
a summer field would be best of all,
but ah, that's the commercial. Love...
she'll gaze with unslaked eyes
through its glowing window.

WHAT'S FINE

Romantic lovers sigh when silks
go hempen...when the brightest hair
turns straw...when veins glare blue through skin
radical for oxygen.

But others take their weather harsh,
inspired by strength and perishing
from plush. They image delicacy
as a movie star, rice-powered, in

her mansion, pale her hangings, sad
and pale. For them the full-mouthed singer
glories, and Great Pan with hooves,
with horns and matted fur, transcends

the grace of cavalier. The gauzes
rise; the music's blue; the Swan
arrives; Pan grips her—lovely—lifts her,
holds her.

DIM SUM

I know, I know, if Ernest Hemingway
had savored the chicken bits
in piquant sauce
at the great Dim Sum Restaurant
in Monterey Park, California, he
still would have...could have...

or if Richard Brautigan
toward the withered end
had paused for the scallops at the Dim Sum
or ordered the platter of three
huge cream-filled dumplings, still he—
I know, I know, stupid thought,

but if only
John Berryman...Anne Sexton...
if Sylvia Plath...Primo Levi...
if Kathryn's father...
Robert Hazel...
if Marilyn Monroe....

FROM THE 40TH FLOOR

New York morning, 4 a.m.:
feel it roll, the cumbersome world?

Sparse traffic moves through mist of rain:
orange passage of waterlights.

A horn blares out as if from above—
hovers—brazen annunciation.

The very buildings seem to tilt,
as of course they do, continually,

shifting their bones the slightest bit,
like lovers carefully turning.

YOUNG LOVERS

Each time I brought her home from the movie
is Poppa and Momma waiting, watching:
Momma who claimed to like me, meaning
cakes and chat and coffee, Poppa
slugging his beers—he never could wait me
out, at last had to leave the TV
to us, no hope I'd go home early
even once. Exhausted, he knew
exactly what we would be up to
as soon as he rose from *Playhouse 90*.

Poppa, I would have waited if need be
through *Sunrise Semester, Today,* doomsday,
to huddle with her on that creaky couch,
serious at our own Playhouse
alone at last to our *Show of Shows*
whispering of vast time ahead,
no Poppa blear-eyed on Barka Lounger,
no Momma to call down "Has he left?"—
iris in a silver vase:
music: moonlight: a four-poster bed.

THE ZEN MASTER'S MOTHER BIDS FAREWELL TO HER THINGS

He took her for a visit home
from the Home, for this was her great desire.

Given cataracts, she failed to see
the dust that occurs in an empty house,

but the missing she saw, and the out-of-place:
it belonged at the top, not the lower shelf,

her silver epergne on the serving cart;
and where in the world was her little bell,

had they stolen her precious Sevres bell
wherewith one alerts the kitchen-girl?

"We are ready for the soup now, Gussie."
And now even Gussie had stolen away.

Her things and her self seemed one and the same.
He thought she would be as much concerned

with a severed toe or a straying hair
as the loss of her dollhouse Persian rug.

He followed her from room to room:
they never did find the blue Wordsworth

where her father had pasted her Lake Country sketches,
gone, gone, as she would be.

Goodbye little things, she seemed to say.
Goodbye little body and little life.

Later he joked that he'd made a new vow:
from his last chopsticks-pair to give one stick away.

And yet he loved her, and yet he wept
that all refused to go on as she'd have it,

forever; that all must forever go on and on.

SONG FOR WOODEN FLUTES

Ill at ease in the living room,
as if we'd invented the whole world's woe,
all's wrong, wrong, we sway and mourn:
imagining badly, we'd made it so.

Yet always like earth we'll lumber on,
like air and water flow, though we yearn to be
fire, our music
its mimicry.

Meandering like the sinuous sound
of wooden flutes that greet the dawn
we've chosen roads that get us lost,
who are each other's coming-home.

BIO

Feeding the jukebox in gravelly truckstops,
or sparking the maidens, swirled cape and cane,
I wanted a life filled with aunts and uncles,
to prosper without an enemy
through Garbo-Thrift-Shop-Bugatti-charm.

On my wall hung a photo-postcard of "Jo,"
delirious girl-child riding a sow
in Nineteen Three, meant to signify
careless wisdom mastering flesh,
the moment dancing: rut, and bliss.

My bowl holds seventeen champagne corks;
I never expected to count the losses,
how life runs to ruin, a Trojan palace,
its Helen-porches crumbling daily,
weird props maintaining the odd green limb.

Now quietness comes to nest in my dwelling
and there I brood on the work of the stars,
how they pulse toward whatever has need of them;
how they selflessly spend their offerings
from light-years and light-years away.

WORRYING THE MUSE

You used to come nightly, kick off your heels,
hum in my ear—how my atoms purred
from the way that you laugh
when you're cheating at Scrabble!

I know, our deal: no questions asked,
no fits if you lurch in from partying
with whole translation committees. Sure,
no one's about to love you tame,

but look—how abject can I get?—
the study's dusted, quiet, I've set
cornflowers on the desk, our favorite
pad and pen...whatever helps.

Did you just get too damn lonesome for
Tangiers, or Massachusetts snow?
No, tell, tell...
is there someone else?

AH LA

I'm walking State Street when this bare-armed girl
comes fetching up beside me at a light,
a lovely Oriental-looking letter
tattoo'd on her fine arm below the shoulder.

I ask her if the tattoo'd mark is Sanskrit—
"Arabic."—we're crossing—"It's for "Ah la!"
which brings a smile, until I hear her: "Allah."
"It's beautiful," I offer from the heart.

"Thank you"—there's a tremor to her voice—
"thank you…very much." Her tall young life
is filled with every grace, and yet it seems
she hasn't heard of beauty near enough.

I turn, I nod and smile and wave goodbye
letting the distance lengthen then between us
as one who'd chanced to pay a passing reverence,
and she uncertain, in her glory days.

SOMETIMES A WOMAN

Sometimes a woman needs kind eyes upon her.
Home from work she "tells her day":
lunch at *The No Name*, high gulls at bayside,
a meanness, a triumph, a hard decision,
a sign on the pier reading "DEEP DEEP OCEAN
FISH CO." Deeply her eyes are green
and you enter into that deep deep ocean
as summer increases, northward from Spain.

AT THE DOOR

I ring her bell in the cold, admiring
through cataract-frost the plants in her window.

She'd led a difficult life, this woman
moving toward me: had known despair,

so savors pleasures, seeing that trouble
serves itself each day like air.

Smiling-eyed she opens the door
biting into a winter apple

and I recall a photograph:
a hospital, a Chinese woman,

acupunctured, amazingly munching
an apple as she views in a mirror

medical gloves at work in her open
heart. My friend stands, laughing-eyed,

munching on her apple, and I—
for once for sure I see her.

"THERE'S NO MORE OF ME"

Aunt Helen weighed forty pounds when she died
and did not know her name or place on earth.

"There's no more of me," she whispered—
ninety years and forty pounds, imagine,

my aunt, a cause of my lifelong love
for the fiercely sweet intelligence

of women: a woman who never forgot
birthdays, phone numbers, could recite

the capitals of every state,
the Presidents, forward, backward. Once,

entirely tall and elegant,
her eyes the blue of tentative dawn,

she'd tease me not to gaze in mirrors—
"You'll freeze into that face!"—explained

why only her oatmeal tasted so good:
"I mix it with my thumb"—who revealed

(a strap slipped) to this boy, amazed,
an instant of shying breast, her body

shrunken, shrunken her sprightly mind
drifting inanely into non-being

who'd let me iron her bedsheets for her,
who taught me how to waltz.

47

IMAGE

Once I felt like a rodeo bull,
snorting, enraged, boxed-in by gates
that an easing latch might open at last...
and then? I expected to leap beyond pain,
magically free of the tightened strap
at the groin...but instead came human weight,
the intent of my designated rider,
and all my terrible bucking.

BY CANYON CREEK

I trek alone through snowy woods,
the movement of the laden branches
as easeful as a sleeper's nodding.

Waterfall-strands seem motionless
so far away, but closer by,
below the creek's bright water-chatter,

comes constantly a fall's big sound
which is where these small
young sounds are going.

For hours I keep to the trail alone,
brush of pine-needles, boots crunching snow,
and then in the distance a woman approaches,

smiles as she passes, no words between us,
her sureness among the lodge-pole pines
so beautiful that for a time

all world-dread's gone. I pause to write
on pocket paper. Three hunters' shots
hardly jitter my pen or my freezing fingers.

THE BLIND GIRL AT THE BUS STOP

Smiling behind her mirror-glasses
she asks which bus is pulling in.
The 24...not hers...her dog
leads her back under eaves into shade,
a pretty dark-haired girl, so placid,
settled on the bus stop bench.

I'd noticed her before, at a dance,
without the dog, with a handsome boy
who'd led her gracefully out to the floor
with the lightest conceivable touching of fingers;
reggae music; her hair done "soul,"
in bead-braids.

Now I see myself
small in the silver of her glasses.
I wait at the end of the line, I mount
my bus. She's smiling out of her darkness.
The dog sits, and she touches its head
with a touch like the handsome boy's.

I carry it with me, that smile.
At home
I experiment, I close my eyes,
becoming her, my own quenched self
as vast as the unrelenting dark
she has no choice but to trust.

BLACK STAR YEARNING

Black-star yearning, old heart grinder,
nothing to do but to sweat you out,
tear up the list of urgencies,
fold the long legs of the day.

Evening again. A school of starlings
swirls the sky like a dreamed explosion
and wildflowers flare my speeding windshield
briefly, yes, but unspeakably blue.

O, star-meat! O, incarnate source,
shatter my iron parentheses!
Though often I stall, like the undropped shoe
I'm still held in my own friendly hands.

Blessed are those whose work is presence:
dogs by the sea so joyful they're teachers...
donkeys who move like little mothers...
people so strong they risk being kind.

The air provides: it feeds the breath.
There is no sun that lacks for light.
Blind blossoms can't see their colors glow.
In unwillable ways we are beautiful.

PEACHES & CREAM

You bring me
peaches and cream

in a crystal dish
with a silver spoon.

The taste of the peaches!
The weight of the spoon!

The cream the way
it covers the tongue!

Peaches and cream
in the morning arriving

you smiling me sitting enormously
awake in the rumpled bed.

III.

NEWS FROM THE ICE HOUSE

Summer will stream in rivulets,
asters surrounding the Ice House. Water—
how placidly as ice
it waits for freedom.

Love in its essence is boundless; here,
with us, it moves by ebbs and floods,
in tides. Etched in the Ice House window:

"ELIZABETH ETERNALLY, 2/17/04"

Wistfully Elizabeth
forms me a kiss through rime-dimmed glass.
Easy loving fantasies
a camera'd film through gauze,

but how to bear our beer-sad fathers?
wives who ululate and keen?
the cussed hopes and miseries
of familiars?

The thought of a once-loved friend
throbs like an amputated limb.
"Elizabeth Eternally,
2/17/04."

PAWN

Not yet aware of the end-game's amazements
a woman once told me she'd spent half her life
as a lowly pawn, patient foot soldier
steadfast among the jazz-dance Horses
guarding a Castle that weighed down the field.

But then came firestorms, few survivors
attending the King in his mid-game crisis,
she marching on toward original force,
advancing rank after rank, transformed

to Omnipotent Queen, Undeflectible Whirlwind,
this small one, ignored through so much of the action,
who'd shivered before with the grunts in the trenches.

RESCUING THE MAIDEN

Below the tower you find her shoes...
what dainty feet could fit in those?
A clue, thrown down!—she's trapped up there
where the Ogre has his way with her
hourly: huge, he leans on his club,
then spreads her out on the towerstones.

Razorswift you start your climb,
self-chosen Hero, jut by niche,
rising—horror grows like fur:
enormous monster, girl so small....
A scream bloodshrills above, but you
must pause for breath, newt on the wall,

strengthless as you view below
the Ogre's fields: carts heaped with straw;
workers, slave and miniature;
the distant hills of hermitage.
The scream again! You climb, and as you
straddle the battlements come to know

full dread: you're there without a weapon,
with only your need to rescue the maiden.
The Ogre appears, his skin disease
like polyps of oozing seaweeds...he's
alone! Immense, he mimics the sound
of violated delicacy,

then over the battlements glides away,
laughing, sighing maidensigh,
down the tower as blue groans rise,
smoothing to human form again.

"My substitute's arrived!" he cries,
and all the pretty farmers run

to give him love—his term is done,
his time of striving to rescue the maiden.
Now you're the holder of the tower,
feeling your monster-nature flower...
Hero-Ogre, how you mourn!—
you practice solitary moan,

and, finding scrap-hide on the stone
—what other stratagem to use?—
you start to craft two tiny shoes.

THE RODIN OUTSIDE THE WELLESLEY COLLEGE LIBRARY

Headless, yes: a huge, heroic
torso, without intellect
or feature: fundamental Earth.

No arms as well...a gentled crotch
bronze-blurred to unisex (a joke
to the rare males in this female place).

Could he be randy Hercules,
or Zeus, our stiff-necked amorist
who made Alcmena's nights, who bellowed with Europa,

here modeled as a girl?
And the women, do they pass him unoffended?
I know some see an image stark and coarse,

a tease from tough Rodin, that shameless lover,
a presence in this absence of a penis
by which a cruder thought's set loose

as through some convoluted verbal engine
ideas are thrust upon us in a poem
by Cowley, say, or Donne—

for he can strike the eye as one huge member,
one great dark phallus, striding forth on legs,
tumid in the middle of the campus.

Yet others choose to read him as a wound
here healed by art for once, requiting sorrow—
a mollifying wholeness, pacified,

and all of us one body, as we are,
and all our bawdy battles quieted,
the hard complaints of Hera.

SATURDAY WEDDING

One restless night in a Psycho motel
shower steam rescrawled a mirror-note:

"Linda: forgive me, I couldn't—Hal."
What did Linda want? Why did Hal cop out?

Hard sacrifice, performed in silence?
Some sort of Liebestodic finish?

The woes of lovers! Cars drive State Street
decked with flowers—the bride's blonde hair

nearly angel-white, from the love of the sunlight,
the groom in triumph, smiling, smiling;

onlookers cheering; car horns blaring...
all of creation, St. Francis assures us,

is meant for human joy. Most creatures
will not eat, some even may aid

another of their kind.

PORTRAIT IN ONE SITTING

She's planting her someday-perfect herb garden—
every spring she plans it anew—

and if I question her now I know
her answer will climb slow stairs to reach

her lips, or hover unsaid in her smile,
the Cheshire-cat-like evidence

she's crossing the border into light,
common sprig or rare in her hopeful hand.

SCAR

In sixth grade, Lenny Weinstein and I,
we were Miss Schnell's two "big boys."
"Where are my big boys?" Miss Schnell would say,
as if we weren't at it already
pushing hard at the top of the stuck
window only we could raise
on muggy days, so she had us believe,
her big boys.

Then came a time when Lenny, out sick,
missed school, so I strained at the window alone
and shattered the glass I pressed against,
slitting my wrist. My pollywog scar
has been taken by some as a remnant sign
of a suicide-quest, not my hero's intent
to triumph, proving my manly blood
as one of Miss Schnell's two big boys.

I dripped dark blood down the stairs at school
as Louie the Janitor followed along
patiently with his mop. Miss Beatie,
Assistant Principal, bound me up.
They whisked me off to Dr. Wallen's,
eight stitches, my scar, my badge of honor
noted by Sylvia Plath shaking hands
at a Fulbright Fellows' reception at Cambridge.

They glittered, she and Ted, just engaged.
She took in my scar, so I told the story,
no claim of membership in the club
she knew the secret handshake of.
Often I've thought how she'd held my hand

to view the wrist-slit scar I got
from hoping to shove a window up,
one of Miss Schnell's two big boys.

STUNT MAN

Come to earth safely, A.J. Bakunas;
descend, reborn in angelic slowness
your two hundred eighty eight feet in Kentucky.
You tried to leap from a higher height
than your rival the Guinness Book record holder
and broke the bag that cushions stunt falls.
"Look, Ma, no hands!"—and then, straight through her.

When you return, take female form,
grieving a while on the man you'd been,
the pride and the cost of a life as Bakunas...
understanding the boyish passions,
the dance on the edge in a solitude
that blinds; the need to prove, and to prove;
those stunning, ardent, fall-busted bones.

A STRANGER

I took the wrong briefcase, its papers in German;
its owner had mine, filled with English. We met,
happy to switch, and she said, in her accent:
"I almost tell you I love you."

We made exchange. For the briefest moment
her wrist dwelt in my hand. Since then
I've held dear others, scrawled much English
on hopeful pages, and to this day

can summon her whenever I wish
by the sense of her narrow wrist in my circlet
of fingers—a stranger whose words I'd returned;
who almost told me she loved me.

A SUMMER HOUSE

This summer house, a refuge house
for out-of-season lovers, locked
through the dead of the year, yet somehow they manage
to open the place, and one another.

I think of a couple against a wall
in zebras of moonlight; an unsheeted bed;
aroma of wood long breathing itself;
bouy-bell's sound and waves' slow hiss,

slipping clothes and bodies rushed
to love-cry. Then again the house
awaits its owners, who come one morning
and sweat all day in the lower field;

hammerstrokes cross the seaside valley,
and later lights come on in the house
where the lovers had none, nor any need
for light.

SLOWNESS AND APRICOTS

One body, one current, one deepening river,
in languid postures gently together

as sugar works in banana skin,
dark, unspeakably we ripen,

by mute intelligence of flesh
fierce and delicate at once.

If nowhere else but in our thoughts
we live on slowness and apricots,

the lovefruits of the Garden: wings
flared and woolly, primal things,

the small earth blinking blue below
where continents and veined valleys flow.

WHAT'S-HER-NAME

My mother had Alzheimers. Fearing combustion
she stacked on refrigerator shelves
her unread evening papers, laughed
to dazzle away forgetting the names
of relatives, friends, discarding at last
her own. I held her hand, unknown,
beside her bed as she babbled on.

With me if it's Alzh it's early, only
suddenly bridgeless synaptic gaps,
connections bombed away. I'll recall
in detail a book I read years before
or the layout of Barson's Drugs where I soda-
jerked at age fifteen, but not
some actor's or entertainer's name.

I can see this actress, her subtle beauty,
the delicate wit of her lifted brow.
She stretches her arms in her languorous way,
Ms. Nameless. So I work for recall:
remember some scandal-sheet lie about her,
the dress she wore presenting an Oscar...
maybe she'll whisper her name in my ear?

Names, names, they won't cross the border...!
I'll spend the whole of a Sunday morning
seeking the mock news announcer on *Saturday
Night*, that tumble-down-clown who suddenly...
Cybill Shepherd! Cybill Shepherd!
My God, you can't imagine the comfort,
Dear Cybill, simply to speak out your name.

WEEPER
        for Simms Teramoto

Just because I tend to weep
at funerals, at weddings,

sometimes at well-spiced noodle-dishes;

once while reading Kurt Vonnegut
where he wrote that The Statler Brothers, great singers,
adopted the name of their band from a brand
of paper towels, and once when Julia
Child spent twenty-two pages telling
how properly to prepare french bread,

doesn't mean (recalling Goethe-,
Beethoven-loving Nazis) that I'm

a good guy, just because I weep...
but God, it feels that way!

MORTAL COIL

All of our trouble's from having one life,
only one...I'd rather have many, devoting
year after year to nothing but breathing

(the green-scented air in Brown County,
Indiana, I breathed for a while;
in my breathing-life I'd go back there).

And friends? lovers? listen, my God,
I'd spend an entire life with each
(two with you)—it's many lives

we want, and all at once, only
this one sweet life
will not console us,

this life where we hum
when the soup is thick,
where we cast off our shoes as a greeting and hug

a new friend,
for the very first time,
as if already remembering.

IV.

VALENTINE

I'll usually give you a little poem
and a great big box of chocolates, or
more of a poem and less of a box
and who can say which we'll have except
the chances for chocolate grow smaller word
for word...if this keeps going on
we're down to six fruits-and-nuts, no, less,
three caramels one angelcream watch out
a last Jordan Almond we'd better bite it in
whoops, it's gone, there's nothing left
but you and me, and a yen, I tell you,
heavy for sweets...now what should we do
about that?

PRECIOUS DISASTERS

Our triumphs drift into mist behind us,
but out of the years' long emptying
the errors remain, as if they were precious,
as if they deserved to be fondled, disasters

held in gem boxes lined with plush.
On sleepless nights, press catch after catch
to handle again some stupid choice,
some saddening act still stored undimmed,

the maladroit word that distanced a friend—
the instant before that word was spoken:
her unwarned, beautifully shining face
about to be drained of all light.

TO A LADY

Dear lady, by your fingertips
you rhyme me to a feather.
I run the rapids of your arms
from here to Minnesota.
You sun me bright, you sigh me on
till half of Iceland's burning.
I bless you for your leafy ways.
My breath be all you're wearing.

SPANISH TRAFFIC

The American girl in Barcelona,
she's still angry, four years later,
recalling the Festival of Flowers.

A smiling man had grabbed her up
to run with her in his arms across
an eight-lane highway's Spanish traffic.

It never left his face, that smile
at her curses, at her battering fists,
a smile that says a woman is angry

even when you set her down
across the road where she would be!
That women fight when ruffled, aided,

he's used to that in Spanish women,
rather amused at their enmity,
forgiving their strange ingratitude.

DRIVING TO WORK

He mourns the loss of holy oils,
brilliance that made for profit and pride,

but thinks then how she towels herself
in lace-calmed light at the window, how

her body curves like a bending bow,
her breasts giving mock to gravity,

her hair still wet at the nape and she
is grinning.

THE MUSE

The Muse came pulling off her gown
and nine feet tall she laid her down
and I by her side a popinjay
with nothing to say. Did she mean to stay?

She smelled like flame; like starch on sweat;
like sperm; like shame; like a launderette.
No one, she said, *has loved me right.*
Day and night. Day and night.

ON AN ETCHING BY GUSTAVE DORÉ

The print shows Little Red Riding Hood
beside the Wolf in Grandma's nightgown.
She's wary in that narrow bed
for something's strange, but she's settling down.

The Wolf, meanwhile, who'd meant to consume her,
then lone-wolf-it back to the wild well fed,
as night follows night feels a shift in his humor,
her very presence his daily bread.

It looks like he's moving in for good
as she irons his shirts, bears his wolflets.
Awake in the night he's scheming profits,
passionate to protect her—should

a Woodsman arrive to set her free
he'd rip out his throat! He dotes upon her.
And Little Red—has it made her happy
to own a Wolf because he'd own her?

And Grandma—remember Grandma?—wolfed up
before this domestic transformation
from hunger to thrift?—well, life is tough
even in fairytale translation.

That gaze you get from a wolf: ice blue!
Family Values, "Wolf Makes Good,"
but such long teeth, the better to eat you...
such ancient howling in the wood.

ONE GOOD THING

One good thing I did today
amid various projects and calculations—

I told a woman in sudden need
I'd be "happy as a pear" to help

and she, who'd sounded so desperate before,
laughed on the phone at my words and briefly

there we were laughing, despite all woe,
the two of us happy as pears together.

THE RETRIEVER PUPS

Slick-glazed, color of dawn-in-the-East,
my coffee cup reflects my face
and much of the room in its mirroring blue.
We can't survive without an echo.

Often I'd paw through the bureau drawer
where my mother kept my childhood: bear-
fur photo, Oratorical Contest
Medal, gossamer lock of hair.

We cleaned her out long ago, yet still
I own the cedar-scent of that drawer
where scrapets of me were stored, odd things
already touched with the sadness of loss.

The ten retriever pups, eyes closed,
when their mother leaves for a rest, huddle
beside their substitute mother, the warm
clothes dryer, and cheep, and try to nurse.

AN EARLY MACINTOSH

Rubbing its pectin-gleaming smoothness
I see why new-born Eve might cherish
forbidden fruit: from her wish
for body, for incarnateness,
for just the way this apple fits
to teeth and hand...and even more,
that Adam, too, would eat, for her,
to stay with her, I understand.

WHAT EUGENIA SAID

Eugenia, brilliant hair and eyes,
this is what Eugenia said:

"My father had a heart attack
the day I took him out to lunch
for his birthday. On the sidewalk his heart
exploded, in front of Maxwell's Plum.
I was stunned...he seemed to be trying to smile...
he died before the ambulance came.
These wise guys, kids, they'd stared at us
before, through the restaurant window? My father
loved to tease, he made like to twist
the shortest one's nose off, through the glass.
So he's dying there and they stand around,
they stand around and they look at me—
it wasn't right how they looked at me
and my father dead on the sidewalk."

SWEET OWL

Look, love, how the carver treats
his oak owl: wistful, man and bird,
their foreheads touch, they both wear smiles.

We're charmed to dream, bird beast or human,
that we could live like Pooh, Squirrel Nutkin,
cozy creatures, fur to fur,

when in the real with rapid eyes
we rip, we clutch, *survive, survive,*
deep flyer, my sweet owl.

WHAT'S LEFT

The house of memory clears its burdens...
she hasn't thought of you in years—
wouldn't be able to pick you out
in a naked two-man lineup.

And so, what's left? The thought, like trance,
of how her beauty moved you once;
how you'd blaze and melt, blaze and melt,
at the touch of her lingering hand.

LOVERS ON AN ELEPHANT
after a Jaina miniature

As earth absorbs warmth from the sun
they ride into day out of night,
the last knot of difference undone,
soothed by a wind made of light.

These lovers who never need part,
their weather unendingly fair,
they glow at the pit of the heart,
their curtains like fragrance of pear.

Never to wake from their trance,
their elephant pacing unled,
they rove through the forest by chance,
joined on an animal bed.

They yield up the one pulsing note,
at one in their frail silken room:
ease of the opening fruit;
flowering breath of the womb.

AN ANSWER

Wanting a woman to be comforted, yet saying
just damnably the wrong thing
I came away clotted with failure,
unable to break clear of shame and regret,
baffled by this endless nursing
of wounds taken, given...and received an answer.
Think, said the voice of deeper being,
think of another, of any other,
of the driver who horn-blasts your stupid lane-change;
of the woman disappointed by your lack of grace.

Here is a healing, a magic for you, said this inner-voice.
Think of another, oh it could be not even a person,
grain of the floorboards, dusty TV's face,
bandages on a maimed child.
Think of anyone or anything but self
and the mud-dam that blocks your flowing disappears.
And so it was.
I focused on the woman, not on my mis-speaking;
on the driver, his angry lights high in my rear-view mirror,
and life returned; the woe that had filled me was gone.

But this obsession with triumph runs so deep!—
O Buddha-nature, I said in thought,
I know it will return, my insane
devotion not to fail,
to perform brightly, to be confirmed.
Yes, this is your work, the voice replied.
This is your koan, your problem to solve.
Think of the paperclip on the dashboard;
of the weary man who serves you bread.
So simple, so simple: your problem to solve.

A FORMAL FEELING COMES

Dazed, a woman moves toward safety
covered with the dust of the Twin Towers:
one lone, dignified woman in a photograph,
her eyes maintaining purpose to survive
but with an underglint as from a fear-crazed horse.

This modern person moves
as if through pre- or post-civilization:
in a pants suit, smart purse at her shoulder,
fashionably turned out
for her day in the great city.

The pearls around her neck
spare us an instance of the civilized,
an imagining of hope:
pearls that through it all still yield
their Vermeer gleam.

WITHIN ANOTHER LIFE

Those whose days were grudging or confused
may end up trapped within another life

as a boulder or a pane of glass,
or a door that suffers every time it's slammed.

If I return a boulder, love, some summer day
come sit by me and contemplate these horses and these hills.

And if a windowpane, gaze through to see
the meadow on our walks where brown geese strut.

And if I am a door, come home through me,
be sure I'll keep you safe.

And if a knotted, twisted rope
from long self-clenching and complexity,

oh love, unbind, unbraid me then
until I flow again like windswept hair.

Barry Spacks, after many years of teaching at M.I.T., now earns his keep as a writing and literature professor in the English Department and the College of Creative Studies at UC Santa Barbara. He has published poems widely in journals paper and pixel, plus stories, two novels, and (as of late 2004) nine poetry collections, the most extensive of which is *Spacks Street: New And Selected Poems* from Johns Hopkins. He has a CD out, "A Private Reading," presenting 42 poems selected from 50 years of poetry-work.